TELEPHONE SKILLS FROM A TO Z

The Telephone "Doctor"® Phone Book

Nancy J. Friedman
THE TELEPHONE "DOCTOR"®

A FIFTY-MINUTE™ SERIES BOOK

CRISP PUBLICATIONS, INC.
Menlo Park, California

TELEPHONE SKILLS FROM A TO Z

The Telephone "Doctor"® Phone Book

Nancy J. Friedman

Telephone "Doctor"® and Business Friendly® are registered servicemarks of The Telephone "Doctor" Inc.

CREDITS:
Editor: Carol Henry
Layout and Composition: Interface Studio
Cover Design: Carol Harris
Artwork: Ralph Mapson

English language Crisp books are distributed worldwide. Our major international distributors include:

CANADA: Reid Publishing, Ltd., Box 69559–109 Thomas St., Oakville, Ontario Canada L6J 7R4. TEL: (905) 842-4428; FAX: (905) 842-9327

Raincoast Books Distribution Ltd., 112 East 3rd Ave., Vancouver, British Columbia, Canada V5T 1C8. TEL: (604) 873-6581, FAX: (604) 874-2711

AUSTRALIA: Career Builders, P.O. Box 1051, Springwood, Brisbane, Queensland, Australia 4127. TEL: 841-1061, FAX: 841-1580

NEW ZEALAND: Career Builders, P.O. Box 571, Manurewa, Auckland, New Zealand. TEL: 266-5276, FAX: 266-4152

JAPAN: Phoenix Associates Co., Mizuho Bldg. 2-12-2, Kami Osaki, Shinagawa-Ku, Tokyo 141, Japan. TEL: 3-443-7231, FAX: 3-443-7640

Selected Crisp titles are also available in other languages. Contact International Rights Manager Suzanne Kelly at (415) 323-6100 for more information.

Library of Congress Catalog Card Number 94-68081
Friedman, Nancy J.
Telephone Skills from A to Z
ISBN 1-56052-301-8

This book is printed on recyclable paper with soy ink.

ABOUT THIS BOOK

Telephone Skills from A to Z is not like most books. It has a unique "self-paced" format that encourages a reader to become personally involved. Designed to be "read with a pencil," there are exercises, activities, assessments and cases that invite participation.

This book is to be used as an informational, reference-type book. It can also be used as a training tool. But unlike some textbooks, this book should not be read and then ignored. It's designed to serve the reader on an ongoing basis . . . consulted often for both information and support!

—**Individual Study.** Because the book is self-instructional, all you need is a quiet place, some time and a pencil. Completing the activities and exercises will provide valuable feedback, as well as practical ideas for improving your business telephone-use skills.

—**Workshops and Seminars.** This book is ideal for use during, or as preassigned reading prior to, a workshop or seminar. With the basics in hand, the quality of participation will improve. More time can be spent practicing concept extensions and applications during the program.

—**College Programs.** Thanks to the format, brevity and low cost, this book is ideal for short courses and extension programs.

There are other possibilities that depend on the objectives of the user. One thing is certain: even after it has been read, this book will serve as excellent reference material that can be easily reviewed.

ABOUT THE AUTHOR

Nancy Friedman, the Telephone "Doctor"®, has been setting the standards for telephone skills and customer service for thousands of corporations in the United States and abroad for more than ten years. Telephone "Doctor"® videos are available in seven languages and in 27 countries.

Nancy is regarded as "America's foremost and most sought after speaker on customer service and telephone skills." She and her husband, Dick, work together at their new Telephone "Doctor"® headquarters building in St. Louis, Missouri.

Nancy can be reached at:
The Telephone "Doctor"®
30 Hollenberg Court
St. Louis, MO 63044
Phone: 314-291-1012
Fax: 314-291-3710

DEDICATION

This book is dedicated to several people. First, to my husband, Dick Friedman, for his constant support, love and understanding. And to my children, David and Linda, and their spouses, Robyn Friedman and Les Steinberg. Their humor lends significant insight.

To the entire Telephone "Doctor"® and Weatherline® staff who live Telephone "Doctor" techniques daily, illustrating how easy it is to follow them.

To Esther and Arthur Mollner, my parents, and Gerry Mollner, my brother, all now deceased, whose guidance, love and encouragement made me what I am today.

A special mention to Ed Pollock and Margie Allen for their unfailing dedication to and support of this project.

To Charlie Kopetzky whose untimely death was a loss to all who knew him. Charlie wanted me to write this book eight years ago, with the title, *Are You Able to Hold?* I can still see his head going back with laughter when I think of that time.

PREFACE

This isn't brain surgery. We're not trying to cure cancer. We're just trying to be nice to others when they call ... and when we call out. Let's not make it more difficult than it is. To get the most out of this book, we recommend you underline or highlight those skills and techniques you want to utilize.

It's common sense ... and unfortunately, not practiced enough, as we all know.

We've taken the most important skills, tips, ideas, and techniques and put them in this book. In the future, electronic technology will change, but the all-important people skills—the contents of this book—is timeless. Being friendly to the caller *before* you know who it is will never go out of style.

So enjoy, and remember the Telephone "Doctor"® motto:

"IT'S FUN TO BE GOOD!"

Nancy Friedman

Nancy J. Friedman

Telephone "Doctor"® improving the performance
on the phone.

CONTENTS

CONTENTS (continued)

INTRODUCTION

"Your people stink …"

With those succinct words, Telephone "Doctor"® history was born.

Ten years ago, I called my insurance agent after being treated rudely, and told him, "Your people stink!" He asked me what happened and I told him. "Your people are so rude, so unhelpful, so unfriendly, so discourteous. I don't want to do business with you anymore."

He understood. "You know, Nancy, you're right. When I call your office, I'm treated like a king, and I'm not even a customer."

I told him that we treat our wrong numbers better than he treated his customers.

Then he asked me to come over and show his staff what we did at our office.

I went to the agent's office and stood up in front of 10 to 12 people around a table—their pen and paper ready for some scientific strategy on how to be nice on the phone. Would you believe, when I told them at our office, we say "Thank you" and "Please," they stopped to write down those words? That's right. They thought thank you and please were good ideas!

I spoke with them for about 20 minutes and when I was leaving, the president of the agency stopped me and told me "Thank you, we really learned some new things!"

Dazed, I came home to my husband, Dick, and shared the story with him. "The president of the insurance agency told me that he 'really learned some new things,'" I said. "I don't understand." Dick told me, "Don't be surprised, Nancy. Nobody's ever shown them."

I mentioned this story to the general manager of a newspaper in Davenport, Iowa.

INTRODUCTION (continued)

The next day, he called me and asked me to come up to his newspaper and train his people, because, as he said: "If there's a telephone on anyone's desk, they should be trained!"

I wrote a half-day program, flew up to Davenport and delivered the program four times. The first was to management only, because, as the general manager said: "If this program is to work, and I want it to, it must start at the top. It must dribble down. It can not dribble up."

After this first program, the paper's editor came up and told me: "Nancy, that was fabulous. You're very good. You sure have all the cures, don't you?" And he snapped his fingers, pointed at me and said: "You're the doctor … you're the Telephone 'Doctor'."

I told my husband that I had been dubbed the Telephone "Doctor"®. "What do you think?" I asked. He replied "We should get it registered, because we're going to have some fun!" And fun we've been having, traveling the world, and prescribing cures for telephone ills.

SECTION

I

ATTITUDE: IT'S YOUR CHOICE

We have little or no control over many things in life, but we *do* have control over one essential quality: our attitude. Disinterested, bored, unmotivated people aren't very productive, and they achieve little satisfaction in life. In contrast, people who make an effort to have a positive and cheerful attitude typically reach many of their goals, and they usually are happier and more fulfilled!

Successful people normally have made two decisions about their attitude:

1. I can control my attitude! A cheerful and positive attitude can be created, with practice and hard work. First of all, it requires belief in the fact that a positive attitude determines the quality of your life as much as any other single factor. Controlling your attitude demands dedication, and a commitment to creating this attitude.

2. I will make the workplace an ideal site for me to use my cheerful, positive attitude! You spend a good percentage of your life in the work environment. But each week has a total of 168 hours. If you work full-time, you're only at the office about 40 hours—that's less than 25 percent of your week. So we're not asking for an awful lot of time to be positive.

How you perceive and function in your workplace is key to creating a cheerful, positive attitude in every facet of your life. Any job can be boring … or it can be exciting and fulfilling. Your attitude will make the difference. Take each task and do it well, one step at a time. With a positive attitude, work will become fun. And you'll feel good about it—and about yourself, your co-workers and your company.

So, yes, attitude is a matter of choice. It can be controlled, and doing your job well can become the basis for a positive attitude in your personal life, as well.

Attitude: It's Your Choice (continued)

℞

There is a wonderful saying: "Once a job has first begun, never leave it till it's done. Be the labor great or small, do it well or not at all."

If you're going to do something anyway, you might as well do it with a smile and make it fun.

Exercise: Attitude: It's Your Choice

1. Why do you think it's important to have a cheerful, positive attitude?

____

____

2. Name three things you can do to improve your attitude toward your job.

____

____

3. When do you believe would be the best time to dedicate yourself to improving your attitude?

____

____

BE FRIENDLY BEFORE YOU KNOW WHO IT IS

see also "Six Cardinal Rules of Customer Service"

Has this ever happened to you? You telephone a company and are treated in a fairly average manner. Then, the person with whom you're speaking realizes you're a friend of the boss or someone other than an average customer, and they brighten up! Why discriminate? Every customer is a form of job insurance *for your job*! If you're friendly *before* you know who it is, you're giving the same good service to everyone. That's the way it should be. Treat *every* caller as though he or she is special. Every call is unique.

Some people who answer phone calls treat people they know (and like) very pleasantly, but "ordinary" callers get ordinary treatment. Why can't they answer the phone in a friendly way all the time? Why do they handle some calls—personal ones, for instance—with one attitude, and calls from customers with another attitude?

"Well," they say, "some calls are more fun. When my friends call, for instance. Business calls are … well, just business. It's not like it's a conversation or anything. I just want to be efficient."

Efficiency is a worthy goal, but you needn't sound like a human answering machine! With so many of today's calls being answered electronically, it's more important than ever to show your personality on every call. Be friendly to every caller *before you know who it is*. In doing this, you will avoid discriminating between two types of callers in your mind: family and friends, who get friendliness; and customers, who get unfriendly "efficiency."

The person who first answers the phone is the company "greeter," setting the mood for the call. Callers mirror how they're treated. If you are friendly, they tend to be friendly. If your attitude is cool, very likely they will reflect that coolness back to you. A good reception implies a good company; a poor reception, a poor company.

Remember, your callers *are* your friends; they're your *business* friends! Renew your enthusiasm often, and rededicate yourself to being *Business Friendly®*.

Exercise: Be Friendly Before You Know Who It Is

1. Can you tell when someone you call is friendly before answering the phone?

____

____

2. In what way can efficiency interfere with friendliness on the phone?

____

____

3. Why are business callers your friends?

____

____

BUFFER WORDS

see also "Three-Part Greeting"

Here are some sample buffer words:

Good morning.
Good afternoon.
Thanks for calling.
Happy Holidays!

You do it in person, don't you? When you go up to someone at a party on Saturday night, you stick out your hand and say, "Nice to meet you" or "Good to see you" or "Hi, my name is Lee, what's yours?" Those are all buffer words to warm the relationship. Why not do the same on every telephone call?

Rx

Buffer words precede and set up the most important part of the greeting, which in most cases is the company name and/or the department name.

BUREAUCRATIC BOUNCE

You're calling a government office, an organization, an association—any office with more than two floors—and you have this experience:

1. First, you get the operator: *"Hello, Acme Insurance."*
You: *"Yes, I'd like to talk to someone about a change of address."*
"Address change? Oh, well I'm not sure … hold on."

2. Then, the next voice: *"Hello, may I help you?"*
You: *"Yes, I'd like to have you change my address."*
"Oh, well, I don't know how to do that. Hold on."

3. Then, the third voice: *"Hello."*
You: *"Yes, I'd like to talk to someone there about changing my address on your records. I'm not getting your mail."*
"Oh, well, I don't handle address changes. Let me see if I can find someone. Hold on."

BUREAUCRATIC BOUNCE (continued)

4. Then, the first voice again: *"Hello."*
You: *"Yes, can you help me have my address changed?"*
"Oh, it's you. Didn't anyone help you yet?"
"No, that's why I'm still on the line."

"Well, I'm not sure who can help you. But I think the lady you need to speak to is Mary Smith. And she's not in today. She should be in tomorrow. Try then, okay?" Click!

The Bureaucratic Bounce has to be the absolutely worst example of ineffective telephone service! It happens all the time, and that's unfortunate—because the solution is simple: **job knowledge!**

Yes, job knowledge—knowing your job and knowing your company—is the cure for the Bureaucratic Bounce. No matter what your caller wants to know about your company, your firm, or your organization, your answer should be: "That's a good question. Let me check and find out." Because you *will* be able to find out—if you try. You *can* get the information. It's your job, your responsibility, to help the caller once you answer the phone. If you don't know, find out. Help each and every caller.

When you answer the telephone on behalf of your company, you have indeed accepted 100 percent responsibility for the telephone call. Job knowledge and training is the key. Know who the president of the company is; find out the names of the department heads and what they do; be aware of your company's products and services.

Remember, you're on the front line. You're representing the company as well as yourself. Take full responsibility for the telephone call. If you can't provide the answer, get a name and phone number so you or someone else can call the party back. Follow the advice of Telephone "Doctor"®: eliminate the Bureaucratic Bounce with a caring attitude and by knowing your company.

Exercise: Bureaucratic Bounce

1. What do you think is the remedy for the Bureaucratic Bounce?

____

____

2. Why does a caring attitude make a difference in caller service?

____

____

3. Whose responsibility is it when your caller asks you a question?

____

____

CLIFF-HANGERS

TRUE TELEPHONE TALES

Caller: *"Mr. Jones, please."*

Receptionist: *"He's gone."*

Caller, without missing a beat: *"Oh? When did he die?"*

CLIFF-HANGERS (continued)

Replies such as "He's gone," and other one- or two-word answers are called cliff-hangers. They just leave people hanging. Cliff-hangers can be disappointing and frustrating for your callers.

Try not to do that to any caller. Make complete statements. Don't just say "She's not in," or "He's out to lunch." Have an additional backup statement ready.

It's so much more helpful to:

- Offer to take a message
- Offer to help
- Get someone else who can help

Exercise: Cliff-Hangers

1. List two cliff-hangers you have been the recipient of.

   ____

   ____

2. List two cliff-hangers you have used.

   ____

   ____

3. For a cliff-hanger that you have used, rewrite it below to be more helpful to the caller.

   ____

   ____

COMPANY JARGON

see also "Six Cardinal Rules of Customer Service"

Simply put, company jargon should stay in your company. Using it with callers often causes mistakes and miscommunications. You are far more familiar with these terms and abbreviations than the caller, and you won't impress anyone with knowledge they don't understand. Just the opposite—you'll annoy them. To maximize communication and understanding, use common English, without "alphabet soup" abbreviations.

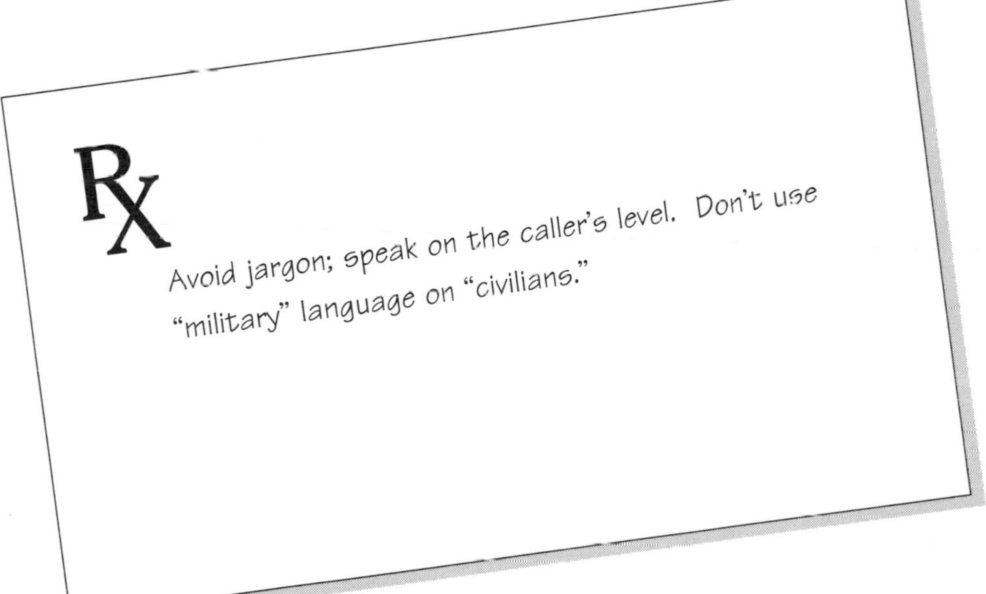

Controlling the Conversation

Callers sometimes shift from topic to topic, or they get carried away on a subject that has no connection to your business or why they called. This may be okay when you have some time and are trying to build rapport on the telephone. However, you usually won't have time for a wandering discussion. Other calls may be coming in, or an important task may require your immediate attention.

What you need to do in this case is *take control of the conversation*. The recommended Telephone "Doctor"® technique is called Back-On-Track. For example, you ask: *"And when do you want us to deliver the bike? We can schedule a delivery Wednesday morning or Friday afternoon."*

"Well, let's see now ... I have an uncle coming in from out of town. He's quite a guy. He's a professional fish guide. His specialty is shark fishing. He was telling us the other day that he landed an 800-pound great white shark. Well, that's not the world's record, I guess, but it took a three-hour battle to land it. Ever go deep-sea fishing?"

Your Back-On-Track response: *"I haven't. And that would be a good reason to have the bike delivered early, wouldn't it? You may even want to ride it before your uncle comes in. Now, would you like to get the bike on Wednesday morning or Friday afternoon?"*

See what happened? By listening, you took control of the conversation by *asking a question*—a related question that steered the caller back-on-track and redirected the conversation.

If you're not able to think of a related question, try this more direct approach: *"Well, that's very interesting, but I know you called to arrange your bike delivery and I want to be able to help you. Which day would you like the bike delivered—Wednesday or Friday?"*

Taking control of the conversation enables you to serve the caller and keep the conversation from wandering, so you don't spend any more time on the call than absolutely necessary.

Rx

Often the most effective route to serving your callers is to help them express what they want and guide them to make a decision. You assist them in getting to the point, so that you can help them. In other words, you serve them by managing the phone call!

Exercise: Controlling the Conversation

1. What should you do with "wandering" discussions?

____

____

2. What's the value of the Back-On-Track question?

____

____

3. What's the one ingredient necessary when controlling the conversation?

____

____

SECTION II

DON'T BE TOO BUSY TO BE NICE

see also "Six Cardinal Rules of Customer Service"

Always be nice, no matter how busy you are. Being busy doesn't make it acceptable to sound rushed, harried or rude. When someone asks you how things are going, say *"Great! How can I help you?"* If you complain about being too busy, you may scare your caller away. The customer wants and deserves all of your attention. If you appear too busy, they may go elsewhere.

For example,

TRUE TELEPHONE TALES

Randy, the owner of a small advertising agency, made it a policy to greet his customers on the phone himself, enthusiastically and warmly, every time. One day he was extremely abrupt and curt to his regular customer, Jo, and she asked if everything was okay. "You're usually so nice," she said. He cut her off to say, "Jo, I'm too busy to be nice today."

Jo didn't call back (and Randy eventually went out of business).

EIGHT GREAT HATES

Several years ago, Telephone "Doctor"® did a survey with *USA Today* to find out what bugs you on the telephone. Being put on hold was the winner. However, there were seven other frustrating events on the telephone. Here are the Eight Great Hates:

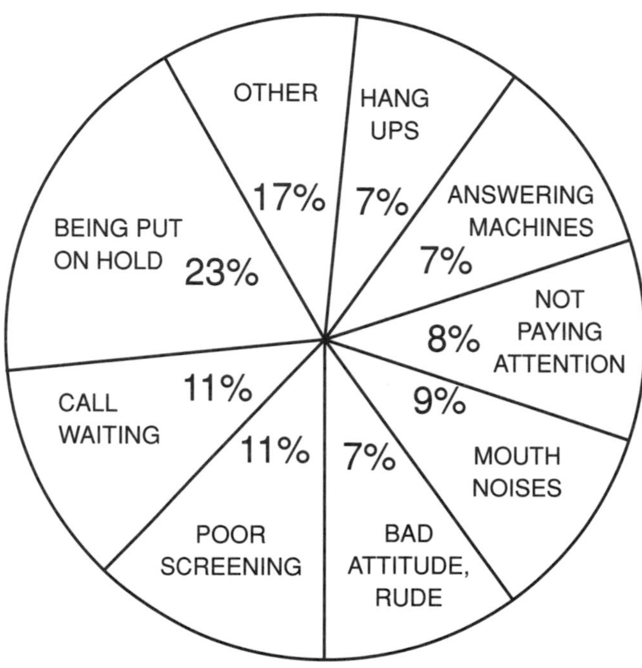

If a survey were taken today, we think voice mail would be high on this list.

Exercise: Eight Great Hates

1. What is your personal "great hate" in telephone calls?

____

____

2. Name three things you can do to eliminate the great hates.

____

____

EMOTIONAL LEAKAGE

"Emotional leakage," in simple terms, is being angry at Peter and taking it out on Paul. In customer service, it's important not to let an earlier negative experience affect your dealings with an innocent caller—somebody who wasn't even involved. It's not right, it's not fun, it's not fair, and of course, it's very rude. But it happens all the time, and often when we're not aware of it!

When something negative happens before that phone rings—you're alone in the office handling all the phones, the computer is down, your car ran out of gas this morning, or the last caller was angry and unreasonable—you need to remember: None of this is the next caller's fault. No matter what your problems are, *it's not the caller's fault.*

It may be especially difficult to remember and accept this when you get a series of complaint calls in a row, and some days are like that. You can almost anticipate another hassle every time the phone rings. But don't let the caller hear that in your voice.

Curing emotional leakage is not that complicated, and these four steps will work for you:

1. **Let the phone ring one more time.** One more ring won't hurt, but answering the phone in an angry mood will. Use this moment to pause and relax.

2. **Take one or two deep breaths.** It's a proven calming influence, one that's recommended by psychologists.

3. **Smile**—Let the smile show in your voice.

4. **Then, answer the telephone.**

EMOTIONAL LEAKAGE (continued)

Rx

Your own previous negative experiences should not affect your phone manners. Successful telephone professionals handle all situations with a positive attitude! They put past annoyances aside, and treat each call as a fresh experience.

Exercise: Emotional Leakage

1. Name one example of when you have experienced emotional leakage.

____

____

2. What's the key thought to remember about emotional leakage?

____

____

3. List the techniques you can use to combat emotional leakage.

____

____

FAST TALKERS

Aggravating, aren't they? Fast talkers are frustrating; however, they can be handled.

Your first instinct may be to yell at the caller and say, "What do you think I am? A recording machine? I can't write as fast as you talk." But hold on to those feelings, and wait for the caller to take a breath—and he or she will. Interject the following: *"Excuse me. I'm having a little difficulty understanding you. If you would please slow down just a bit, I'll be able to get this all correct for you."* It really works! That's what the caller wants: to be assured that you're going to get all the information.

Remember, you don't want to accuse anyone with words such as "Stop going so fast," or "I can't understand a thing you're saying." Those are not caller-friendly words and they won't be appreciated.

FIVE FORBIDDEN PHRASES

The Five Forbidden Phrases were collected from scores of radio and television shows on which Telephone "Doctor"® has appeared. Customers called in and talked about what they don't like to hear on the telephone. Interestingly enough, from California to New York, from Texas to Minnesota, the same five common things annoyed people most.

If you memorize the Five Forbidden Phrases and learn to avoid them, using the recommended responses instead, you will get immediate, positive results.

Forbidden Phrase	*Recommended Response*
1. I don't know	**1.** Gee, that's a good question. Let me check and find out.
2. Just a second	**2.** It may take me a few minutes to get that information. Are you able to hold while I check on that?

FIVE FORBIDDEN PHRASES (continued)

3. No (at the start of a sentence.	**3.** Eliminate it at the start of a sentence.
4. We can't do that	**4.** That's a tough one. Let me see what I can do.
5. You'll have to ...	**5.** What you'll need to do.

Exercise: Five Forbidden Phrases

1. What is your choice for the most irritating forbidden phrase?

____

____

2. Name an additional phrase (to these five) that you wish was forbidden, and offer positive alternatives.

____

____

3. Suggest why the recommended responses are more effective.

____

____

FOREIGN ACCENTS

Call it simple kindness or call it common sense, but learning to deal with language accents that are foreign to you can definitely be good for business. More than one million legal immigrants enter the United States each year, most of whom have one thing in common: English is their second language. These people represent a sizable market for any corporation marketing products or services in the United States. Or perhaps English is *your* second language—in either case, the phone calls you answer may be from people whose accents are unfamiliar to you.

Here are five easy points to remember when dealing with a foreign accent:

1. **Don't pretend to understand.** If you don't understand the person you're speaking with, it's perfectly okay to gently tell them you're having a little difficulty understanding them. Ask them to slow down, so you can get all the information correct. That's what they want to hear. Hanging up without knowing what the caller wants is not good customer service!

2. **Don't rush.** Rushing threatens callers. Take the time—it's usually only a few seconds—to do it right. Listen to the caller's pattern of speech. You'll be able to pick up key words. Repeat the key words back to them—they'll appreciate the fact that you're really listening.

3. **Don't shout.** As the old joke goes … people with accents aren't hard of hearing. Nor do you need to repeat one word over and over, to be sure they understand. Remember, people with an accent usually speak two languages, so it'll take them a little longer to go through the thought processes: their native language for thinking, and English for communicating with you.

4. **Don't be rude.** If you've ever told a caller, "I can't understand you," or "Huh?" or even "What did you say?" you've been a little rude, whether you intended that or not. It's much better to stop, take full responsibility and explain you're having difficulty understanding. Say, "If you'll repeat it for me again, I'll be able to assist you." It's a subtle difference, but a key one.

5. **Do keep a job aid available.** If most of the calls you receive are predominantly from one particular ethnic group, keep a handy JOB AID near your phone—a list with a few commonly used phrases—to get you off the hook. For example, in Spanish *"Un momento, por favor"* means "one moment, please." Even if you pronounce it poorly this would be appreciated by a Latino who's having difficulty trying to say something to you over the phone. You can then pause and bring someone to the phone who can help.

Rx

Making an effort these days to understand and respond to people with language accents is not just common courtesy, it's good business.

Exercise: Foreign Accents

1. Why is dealing effectively with an unfamiliar accent good for business?

___

___

___

2. List the five points that make dealing with unfamiliar accents much more effective.

___

___

___

3. How does a job aid help?

___

___

___

SECTION

III

GETTING A PHONE NUMBER

Let's set the scene:

You: *"Fine, Mr. Smith. Please let me have your phone number and I'll see that she gets your message."*

Mr. Smith: *"Oh, she has it!"*

Ever hear that? And then find that no one has the phone number? Want to have it never happen again? Well, you came to the right place. Use this Easy Reference Technique when asking the caller for a phone number. It works like a charm.

Mr. Smith: *"Yes, please have her call me."*

You: *"I sure will, Mr. Smith. I know she probably has your phone number … but for Easy Reference, would you run it by me one more time?"*

This technique works every time. In the unlikely event that the caller refuses, or insists, "I told you he has it!" and then hangs up, try the white pages, the yellow pages, your Rolodex, Directory Assistance, the computer, or anything else. But try to never deliver a message to anyone without a phone number.

Exercise: Getting a Phone Number

1. Why is it important to get a phone number?

____

____

2. What is the value of the Easy Reference technique?

____

____

3. What can you do if the caller won't leave a number?

____

____

GUM CHEWING

Chewing gum while using the telephone is simply not acceptable. End of subject!

HOLD

Remember, being put on hold won first place in our Eight Great Hates survey. There are two reasons to put someone on hold. You need to have the caller wait while you look:

- For a person
- For information

You'll recall that one of the Five Forbidden Phrases is "Just a second, I'll be right back." And we discussed the proper way to place a call on hold. Let's go a few steps further.

HOLDING FOR A PERSON:

If the person to whom your caller wants to speak is on the phone or temporarily away from his or her desk, rather than keep the caller on hold, try to service the call immediately. It sounds like this: *"Mr. Jones is on another call. I'm not sure how long he'll be?"* The second sentence is important. If you don't say it, the caller will respond, "Well, how long do you think he'll be?"

If you're in a position of strength (a secretary or other assistant, or someone else who can help), use this Service Statement: *"My name is Kyle, I work with Mr. Jones. How can I help you? What can I do for you?"*

Either of these techniques will get the ball rolling and both the caller and the person being called will appreciate it. Everyone gets helped!

If you're on a switchboard and Mr. Jones is taking another call, use this special message-taking technique: *"Mr. Jones is on another call.* ***Let Me*** *have your name and number and I'll see that he gets the message."* Since most switchboard operators don't have time to take long messages, the ***Let Me*** technique does the trick. It's better than asking "Can I take a message?" Getting the name and phone number is preferred, and moves the call along much more quickly.

Today, many companies have voice mail and like to offer the caller the option of leaving a personal message in a voice mail box. But do ask first. Don't just switch the caller unceremoniously to the voice mail system.

By the way, once you take a message, be sure to tell the caller "I'll be sure he/she gets your message." Don't say "I'll be sure to have him/her call you." That's not your job. Your job is to ensure the message gets delivered to the called party.

HOLD (continued)

HOLDING FOR INFORMATION:

Interestingly enough, most people don't mind holding for information as much as for a person.

When someone is calling for information, the Able technique is best. Ask if the caller is "**Able** to hold," give them a visual clue of what you'll be doing to help them, and then wait for a response. You'll usually get immediate positive feedback. For example:

Caller: *"I need to find out about my last payment."*

You: *"Fine. If you're* ***able*** *to hold, I can get you that information. I need to check the computer. Are you* ***able*** *to hold?"*

And then wait for a response. Callers highly appreciate this technique.

RETURNING TO THE CALLER ON HOLD:

When you return to the phone, say "Thank you for holding. I have the information you need." It's only fair, after you've asked if they're Able to hold, that you thank them for holding.

Exercise: Hold

1. Why is being put on hold a most disturbing telephone occurrence?

____

____

2. Name the two types of holds.

____

____

3. In holding for a person, what is the Service Statement, and why is it important?

____

____

4. Suggest why the Able technique is a key to successfully holding for information.

____

____

5. In returning to the caller on hold, what should you say?

____

____

HOW CAN I HELP YOU?

see also "Message Taking Chapter"

A reminder: This service statement is not recommended as an initial greeting. It's suggested for use for someone who has the time and ability to help the caller.

I DON'T KNOW

see also "Five Forbidden Phrases"

There's no need to ever utter these three words. If you don't know, FIND OUT. That's your job. There isn't a thing (outside of sensitive and financial information) that you can't find out if you try.

Use this response, instead: *"Gee, that's a good question. Let me check and find out."* Then go find out.

TRUE TELEPHONE TALES

At a seminar on telephone skill-building, a woman stated that she always tells callers, "I don't know. **BUT** I'll find out." That **"BUT"** was the big eraser—all the caller would hear was "I don't know."

It's important to start this response with a positive introduction, as in "Gee, that's a very good question ... Let me check and find out."

I'M SORRY

Starting a sentence with, "I'm sorry, Ms. Abraham is out of the office," is unnecessary. Use "I'm sorry" only when there's responsibility involved. It's not your "fault" when someone is out of the office. Keep "I'm sorry" from becoming a universal excuse.

It's much more professional, effective, and positive to say, *"Ms. Abraham is out of the office until Tuesday."* Then reintroduce yourself and make your Service Statement (see "Hold"): "How can I help you? What can I do for you?"

When a product or service hasn't been delivered, or you step on someone's toes, that's the right time to say "I'm sorry that happened" and, of course, to make amends immediately.

℞

It's okay to say you're sorry when you step on someone's toes. But you don't need to be sorry when someone is away from the office or is in a meeting.

I.Q. TEST

Circle the letter for the right answer to these questions.

1. How long do you get to make a good first impression on the telephone?
   - a. 4–6 seconds
   - b. 30–45 seconds
   - c. 1–4 minutes

2. What are buffer words?
   - a. Words that add polish to your conversation
   - b. Words that have no specific meaning
   - c. First words of the greeting used in answering a phone call

3. What percent of business calls get completed on the first try?
   - a. 74 percent
   - b. 43 percent
   - c. 25 percent

4. When is a smile most important when handling a telephone call?
   - a. When you greet the caller
   - b. When you state your company name
   - c. Before you pick up the phone

5. When is the customer right?
   - a. When the complaint is legitimate
   - b. Always
   - c. Whenever he or she thinks so

6. When is it okay to hang up on a caller?
   - a. When he or she is rude
   - b. When you know you don't want the caller's business
   - c. Never

7. When can you hear a smile?
   - a. Never
   - b. Always
   - c. On your birthday

8. When should you offer help on the phone?
   a. Only when it's about your department
   b. Always
   c. Only if you have time to service the call

9. When is it okay to lie to a caller?
   a. Never
   b. When your boss tells you to
   c. When you don't know the answer

10. If you call a client and get voice mail, you should:
   a. Hang up immediately
   b. Leave your name, then hang up
   c. Give your name, phone number and a detailed message of why you're calling

I. Q. TEST ANSWERS

Here are the correct answers.

1. **a.** 4–6 seconds. The first indication of a company's excellence is how the phone is answered. It's entirely possible to "turn off" a prospective customer merely by answering the phone tardily, or in a rude or unfriendly fashion.

2. **c.** First words of the greeting used in answering a phone call. Buffer words set up the most important part of any conversation, and are particularly effective when the phone is first answered. Use "Good morning" or "Thanks for calling" before you state your company or department name. Using a friendly buffer makes the caller feel welcome.

3. **c.** Only 25 percent of all business calls get completed on the first try. Find out the best times to reach the person. Make sure to leave a complete message if the party you're calling is unavailable, or use voice mail to leave a personal message.

I.Q. TEST ANSWERS (continued)

4. **c.** Before you pick up the phone. Don't wait to be friendly until you realize it's an important caller on the line. Oftentimes that's too late. If you smile *before* you pick up the phone, you can be sure every caller will get the same warm welcome.

5. **c.** Whenever he or she thinks so. Perception is everything. Customers always think they're right. You'll never win an argument with a customer.

6. **c.** It's *never* okay to hang up on a caller. If you're having difficulty with a caller, ask if they're able to hold and get some assistance. Remember, when you hang up on a person, you label yourself as rude.

7. **b.** You can *always* hear a smile.

8. **b.** *Always* offer to assist the caller. Even if you're not personally able to assist, you can always give the name and the telephone number of the person who can help.

9. **a.** There is *never* a situation when lying to a caller is appropriate.

10. **c.** Leave your name, phone number (repeat it, in fact), and a detailed message of why you're calling. If possible, state a deadline for when you need to be called back. Also, don't forget that most voice mail systems default to an operator. If you prefer, press 0 and see if someone else can help you.

Internal calls

see also "We Are Customers to Each Other"

℞

All callers should be treated equally, whether they are in-house personnel, or outside clients, customers, or consultants.

Irate callers

If your job entails taking calls from unhappy callers, you've got your work cut out for you. Many of us are vulnerable to outbursts from customers or associates who may be dissatisfied with a product or service, or perhaps experiencing a disaster or other stressful situation. Handling these calls takes time and training, but it *can* be accomplished effectively. Here are some techniques for turning unhappy callers into satisfied customers.

IRATE CALLERS (continued)

GET OFF ON THE RIGHT FOOT

Realize that an angry customer is not unhappy with *you*, but with the *situation*. Don't take the caller's hostility personally. You're the lightning rod, not the target.

You can do a great deal to diffuse a caller's anger before you even pick up the phone. How? By *smiling* before you answer that call. A smile really can be heard in your voice over the phone. Your caller will find it more difficult to be rude to someone who's warm and friendly.

USE THE ASAP TECHNIQUE

There are four basic steps to handling an irate caller. We call them the ASAP technique:

- **APOLOGIZE AND ACKNOWLEDGE THE CALLER'S FEELINGS.**
  You'll probably spend about 80 percent of your time soothing the caller and about 20 percent actually working on the problem. Acknowledging feelings is the key: *"I'm sorry the information was incorrect. No wonder you're upset."*

- **SYMPATHIZE WITH THE CALLER. EMPATHIZE!**
  Put yourself in the caller's position; imagine how you'd feel if you were calling with this complaint or problem. You can show your interest in the situation by making statements such as *"I don't blame you for being upset. That's got to be very frustrating."*

- **ACCEPT THE RESPONSIBILITY.**
  When you answer the telephone on behalf of your company, you've accepted 100 percent responsibility for the call. You can say, *"Let's see how I can help. My name is Mary. I'm the customer service manager. And I'm speaking with ... ?"* Always introduce yourself—and if you have a title, now's the time to use it to create credibility!

- **PREPARE TO HELP.**
  Indicate that you sincerely care about the caller's problem. And be sure to use the caller's name—that usually helps to diffuse the anger. Once you've done this, begin to draw out what happened. Then begin to ask questions. *"Thanks, Mr. Jones. Again my name is Mary. Let's see how I can help you."*

DON'T MAKE EXCUSES

Don't make excuses to a complaining caller! No one wants to hear, "The computer is down," or "I'm the only one in the office." That's *your* problem, not the caller's. When you give an excuse, what the caller hears is, "I'm not going to help you now."

AVOID TRANSFERRING THE CALL

Sometimes you won't be able to solve the problem on the spot. Often you'll need more information from another department, or the call may have to be handled by another person. Although these are legitimate courses of action, they will usually upset the caller again.

When you need more information, *tell* the caller that. Ask if they're *"able to hold"* while you obtain it, or if they would prefer to have you call back. Avoid using untrue phrases such as "Hold on a sec." Nothing takes a second.

If you need to transfer the caller, tell him or her the name of the person with whom they'll be speaking. Explain why you're bringing in a third party. *"Joe, Mrs. Smith in our claims department is the real expert in this area. Let me transfer you directly to her. In case we get disconnected, her extension is 431."*

When you contact the person who will handle the problem, be sure to explain it thoroughly. That spares the caller's having to tell it all over again, and perhaps growing even angrier.

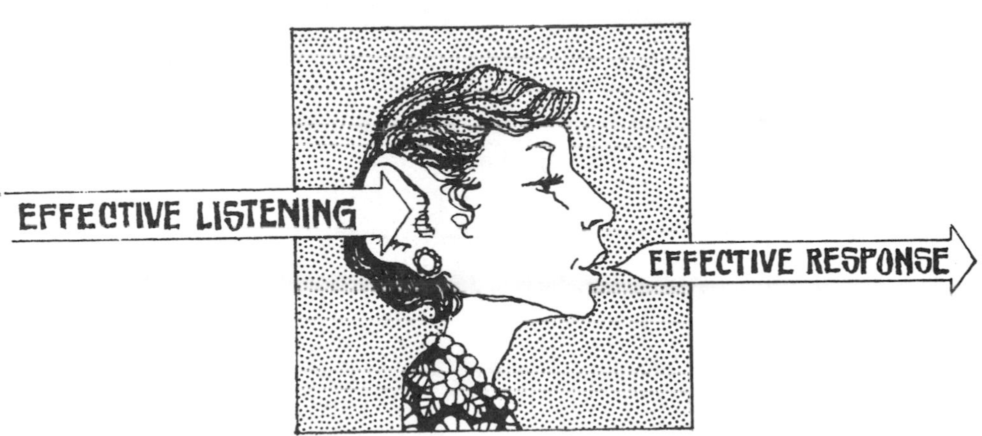

IRATE CALLERS (continued)

Exercise: Irate Callers

1. What two components are part of effectively handling irate calls?

   ____

   ____

2. Why shouldn't you take the caller's hostility personally?

   ____

   ____

3. How can you get off on the right foot when talking to an irate caller?

   ____

   ____

4. Name the four basic steps to take when handling the irate caller.

   ____

   ____

5. When can you use an excuse?

   ____

   ____

6. How can a call transfer be managed efficiently?

   ____

   ____

SECTION IV

JUST A SECOND

see also "Five Forbidden Phrases"

"Just a second, I'll be right back." If you've ever said that to a caller, you've lied. Not a big lie, but nevertheless an unnecessary lie.

Why not tell the truth? *"It may take me a few minutes to get that information. Are you able to hold while I check on that for you?"* This one is a real crowd-pleaser and lessens the pain of being put on hold. Once callers know why they're holding, they're much more willing to accommodate you.

Give a "visual" clue; tell the caller where you're going, so he or she can experience the situation with you. It creates credibility.

Exercise: Just a Second

1. How many times have you been told "just a second," and more than two minutes elapsed?

   ____

   ____

2. What would you do if the caller is calling long distance or is unable to hold?

   ____

   ____

KISS METHOD

The KISS method stands for **K**eep **I**t **S**imple, **S**imon.

As mentioned in the introduction to this book, here we're trying to show how to be *friendlier to people*. This is *not* difficult. It just takes a little time and training—and, of course, observing the Golden Rule: "Do unto others as you would have them do unto you."

LEAVE A GOOD LAST IMPRESSION

We hear so much about making a good *first* impression—and that's certainly important. However, don't forget that leaving a good *last* impression is every bit as important.

Closing a call with "Uh, huh . . . uh huh . . . okay . . . bye" leaves the caller with a feeling of casual dismissal, that they weren't important and you weren't interested. The caller is left disappointed and annoyed.

Instead, try to include some of the conversation in your closing remarks. For instance: *"Yes, I understand. I'll tell Joe and he'll take care of it. He's very good. And we do appreciate your business, Mr. Smith. Thanks for calling. Goodbye."* A remark like that leaves a good last impression!

Here are some other effective phrases to use in closing a phone conversation:

- "Thanks for calling."
- "Please call again."
- "We appreciate your call."
- "Good talking with you."

Don't just let a conversation die. Use your personality to express appreciation for being able to serve the caller. It's an important way to ensure that they will want to call back.

SECTION

V

MESSAGE MANGLING

During an average day, people frequently aren't available to take calls. Taking a message is such a routine task that, often, you might take messages without thinking about them. Or, because you're rushed, the original message might get condensed to a few words or phrases, without many "social graces." Unfortunately, the called party may not get the meaning of the original message, and you might be accused of "message mangling." For instance:

Receptionist: *"John's not here now. Want to leave a message?"*

Tim: *"Yes, I sure do. This is Tim. Please tell him sorry. I'd like to attend the meeting, but I'm unable to. I'm at the hospital, my wife is having a baby. I'll call him tomorrow."*

The receptionist writes hurriedly, "Unable to attend meeting. Will call."

When John reads this message, he gets angry. "What does Tim mean? He can't attend? There's no good reason he can't be there. We planned this meeting last month!"

Tim's actual message explained *why* he was unable to attend the meeting—a justified, self-explanatory reason. Had John heard the original message, he would have understood. Because the receptionist didn't take a verbatim message, the message left was not the message delivered. The message was mangled!

Miscommunication frequently occurs in the business world because of poor message taking. Word-for-word messages are important. In fact, messages should be read back to the caller. That's one reliable way to ensure that the message is what the caller wanted to say! It puts an end to message mangling, especially if you need to abbreviate the message.

Repeat the phone number in pairs of twos, such as: "291-ten-twelve." This lets the caller know you've got it correct.

℞

When you take a message on the telephone, be sure to mark down the date and time, along with all other necessary information. Messages without a date and time have less impact on the person called.

Exercise: Message Mangling

1. Why are messages often mangled?

____

____

2. Why are the dates and times important when taking a message?

____

____

3. Why does repeating a telephone number in pairs of twos help?

____

____

MESSAGE TAKING #1

Why is "Can I take a message?" weak and ineffective? Because the response is all too often, "No, that's okay, I'll call back." And how do you know the caller will? What if he or she needs information right then and there, or need to order something immediately? You can't be sure that this customer won't call a competitor next ... all because of that weak little "Can I take a message?" The cure for "Can I take a message?" is basic, but important: Instead of offering to take a message, offer to help. Be supportive. Be proactive. Create credibility. Here's a sample:

"Mr. Park is in a production meeting until 2:00. This is Mary. I'm his assistant. How can I help you? What can I do for you?" The last two questions are key phrases.

This procedure is much more effective than an apathetic "Can I take a message?" or even "May I take a message?" When you use the "How can I help you?" offer, you're not losing the caller. This is Telephone "Doctor"®'s Service Statement. With it, you're reaching out to the caller!

First of all, you've placed Mr. Park somewhere—perhaps in a meeting or at lunch or at a sales conference. Second, you've reintroduced yourself. (Even if you've said your name in your initial greeting, once you've spoken past that, your name is usually erased from the caller's mind.) Third, you've told the caller your relationship to the called party. And finally, you've used the Telephone "Doctor"®'s Service Statement for message taking: *"How* can I help you? *What* can I do for you?"

Use this message-taking process, and you'll be impressed with how many actual messages you'll write down, and how few of the "Oh well, I'll call back ..." responses you get. The messages you take will be more meaningful, and will translate into better customer service and more sales opportunities!

Every time you're able to help a caller beyond merely taking a message, you make a good mark for your company, for your department, and for yourself. You've been able to serve! And that's exactly what phone calls should be—occasions for service.

MESSAGE TAKING #1 (continued)

Exercise: Message Taking #1

1. Why is "Can I take a message?" weak and ineffective?

 ____

 ____

2. How can you offer to help when taking a message?

 ____

 ____

3. Why does the proactive form of message taking translate into better customer service and sales opportunities?

 ____

 ____

MESSAGE TAKING #2

Picture this: It's 8:30 a.m. You're at a customer's office, pitching hard to keep their business. The pressure's on and you could be out of the office all day.

While you're with your customer, the following scene is taking place at your office: Jane, your assistant, is busily preparing a new business proposal. At 9:05 a.m., the phone rings. The call is for you and Jane says "She's not in. Can I take a message?"

The caller replies, "No, that's okay, I'll call back." Jane, in her nicest voice, says, "Okay, fine, thank you," and hangs up.

Imagine that happening all day long, with all of your incoming calls. Think about Jane's reply. It's 4:00 P.M. You're back at your office and you say to Jane, "Hi, any messages?" Jane says, "Nope, no messages."

But Jane is wrong. She should have had a whole stack of messages for you. Those calls could have been prospects for you, and they may have already called your competitor.

The statement "She's not in ... can I take a message?" commonly used across the country, can cost a firm thousands of dollars in business. This question invites the caller to slip out the back door, by allowing them to respond "No, I'll call back later."

Chances are, there are three or four people in the office who can handle a particular incoming call, or can at least get the ball rolling. Customers are looking for a calm, confident voice to help them. No matter who initially answers the call, that person should assume 100 percent responsibility for handling that call professionally. To a caller who has never seen or done business with your company, the person answering the call *is the company.* That critical first impression can make or break the beginning of a business relationship.

If someone is taking the time to call you, much more is needed than the ineffective "Can I take a message?" What would be better? Here's what Jane should do and say;

Jane Should Do This	*Jane Should Say This*
Tell them where	*"Ms. Jones is out of the office ..."*
Tell them until when	*"... until 4:00 p.m."*
Tell them who you are	*"This is Jane."*
Tell them what you do	*"I work with Ms. Jones."*
Give the Service Statement	*"How can I help you? What can I do for you?"*

How and *what* are the key words. They signal open-ended questions that encourage the caller to talk.

MESSAGE TAKING #2 (continued)

Sometimes, busy switchboard operators cannot afford to give substantial personal attention to a call. There are, however, effective alternatives. See "Hold."

If there's time, a front-line person might also ask, *"If you're able to share a little bit of the nature of your call with me, I can get the ball rolling for you."*

Exercise: Message Taking #2

1. How can the phrase "He's not in . . . Can I take a message?" cost a firm thousands of dollars worth of business?

 ____

 ____

2. In message taking, name two "shoulds" that encourage the caller to talk.

 ____

 ____

Mirror on your desk

see also "Smile"

℞

All Telephone "Doctor"® employees have mirrors on their desks. It reminds them to smile *Before* they pick up the phone.

Music on hold

Let's talk about taped music for callers on hold. Music on hold can be a benefit or a detriment, depending on who's listening. If your company uses music on hold and you're getting a lot of complaints, consider not using it.

Taped announcements are another choice for callers on hold. If you use this to tactfully promote your business and your product, that's certainly proactive, and often a help to your callers. But remember, except when you need to go get more information, callers should not be put on hold for a substantial length of time.

NO AT THE START OF A SENTENCE

see also "Five Forbidden Phrases"

The word *no* at the start of a sentence is unproductive, conveys rejection, and is too blunt.

Sentences can be grammatically correct without the word *no*. But this isn't as easy as it sounds. Turn to the person next to you and say, "Have you ever been to China?" He or she will probably say, "No, I haven't." But it would be just as correct to answer, "I haven't been there yet." That's much more pleasing to the ear.

If you think before you speak, you can turn every answer to a caller into a positive response. Just eliminate the word *no* at the start of the sentence.

What kinds of answers about your company and its business could be improved by using this technique? Here's an example:

Caller: *"Can I get delivery today?"*

You: *"I wish we could. The truck has already left for the day. We can get it for you tomorrow."*

IT'S NOT AVAILABLE IN RED, IS ORANGE OK?

OBSCENE PHONE CALLS

TRUE TELEPHONE TALES

During a recent seminar on telephone techniques, we were discussing how to handle obscene telephone calls. One of the ladies in the audience, a switchboard operator at a very busy company, raised her hand. She said, "I just read them the Bible and they never call back."

Almost everyone at one time or another has received some sort of obscene phone call. They're not terribly easy to handle, whether you're at work or at home. Here are ways to manage them. Perhaps you can think of a few of your own.

1. Change your phone number or get an unlisted number. This is drastic, but it is real action that works.

2. Ask the phone company to put a tap on your phone to try and locate the perpetrator.

3. Keep a whistle by your phone. When you realize you've received a call that offends you, simply blow the whistle into the handset. It's painful for the caller, and it works!

4. Here's the recommended Telephone "Doctor"® technique, which has been approved by police departments. As soon as you hear the obscenities, *gently* (that's the key word, *gently*) hang up the phone or disconnect. *Do not attempt to engage in dialog* with a caller who's using obscene language.

Customers who are very angry and using language offensive to you are handled differently. See "Irate Callers."

OBSCENE PHONE CALLS (continued)

Here's some good news: With the caller ID and call blocking services available from the phone company in some communities, the incidence of obscene phone calls will be decreasing.

Exercise: Obscene Phone Calls

1. What are four techniques to handle obscene phone calls?

___

___

2. Name a basic rule for ending an obscene phone call.

___

___

SHE CORRECTLY HANDLED AN OBSCENE PHONE CALL.

SECTION VI

PEOPLE BEFORE PAPERWORK!

see also "Six Cardinal Rules of Customer Service"

How many times have you tried to talk with someone on the phone while they were obviously doing something else during your conversation? They're going through papers, adding a lot of figures, finishing a note or memo ... maybe you can actually hear papers being shuffled, desk drawers being opened or closed, keys on the computer keyboard being worked. The person talks in a distracted fashion; worse, they ask you to wait while they complete their other task!

Let your paper wait, not your people!

When you pick up the phone, stop whatever you're doing. Put your paperwork aside. It won't disappear, but your caller might! Type or do other tasks only when it pertains to the call.

Acknowledge your callers. Let them know that *they* come first. (They really do!)

Remember: People before paperwork.

PLEASE ... THANK YOU ... YOU'RE WELCOME

see also "Six Cardinal Rules of Customer Service"

"There ya go" is not "Thank you." "Uh-huh" is not "You're welcome."

If someone were to count, starting today, for one day, how many times you say "thank you" and "you're welcome" to your callers, what do you think would be the total number? When a customer has spent money, they want to hear "Thank you. We appreciate your business." And when *they* take the time to say "Thank you," they don't want to hear a mumbled "Uh-huh." "You're welcome" is a pleasant phrase; use it often and don't be a mumbler. Remember to say "Thank you" and "You're welcome."

PUBLIC SECTOR

Those who work in the public sector—in government, public utilities, or other "noncompetitive" agencies and organizations—often have a tendency to believe they do not have a compelling need to serve their callers effectively. (After all, they're not Corporate America; they're the "only game in town"!) In reality, however, nothing could be farther from the truth.

Today, the expectations of taxpayers and utility customers are greater than ever before. Elections, bond issues, public service commission hearings, and the like are barometers of "customer service" quality in the public sector. Serving the requirements of public callers who have urgent questions and need information, or have important complaints, is every bit as important in government as it is in the business community. Public sector employees, as well as private sector employees, need to be concerned with giving good customer service.

If you work in the public sector, how effectively you handle incoming calls is a key to improving the image of your agency. It's important that you understand how to serve the callers in order to play a positive role in customer service. Today, simply having a telephone on your desk gives you enormous customer-service opportunities!

All the skills and concepts and suggestions you will read in this book for improving telephone techniques apply equally to those in both public and private arenas. Good telephone manners are critically important to all of us!

Exercise: Public Sector

1. If it's true that governments and utilities have no competition, why is it important for them to be nice?

____

____

2. Why is effective call-handling important to the image of the public sector?

____

____

3. Do techniques for improving telephone skills apply to the public sector as well as to the private sector?

____

____

QUALITY IS A FOUR-LETTER WORD

We hear so much today about quality this and quality that. But instead of looking at quality as frosting on the cake, let's look at it as something you bake *into* the cake. A basic ingredient.

Quality comes from a four-letter word, and that word is *LOVE*.

There are different types of love. There's the love you have for your mother. You also may love music or a favorite hobby. And there's the love you have for your mate or significant other. Still another kind of love is the love for your job. And people who are out of a job often say, "I'd love to get a job."

There are 24 hours in a day. Seven days in a week. Multiply 24 hours by 7 days and you get 168 hours. Let's take this one step farther. Of the 168 hours in a week, most people work 40 hours. That's one-quarter of your week; 23.8 percent of your week, to be exact, which goes for working. And that 23.8 percent provides you with 100 percent of your pay for all 168 hours.

If you're like most folks, everything you pay for—your mortgage or rent, your family's food, gasoline for your car, breakfast, lunch, dinner, and snacks, a movie or a concert—are bought with the money from your paycheck, which comes from your job. Think about it. (You almost have to be an ingrate not to appreciate your job.)

QUALITY IS A FOUR-LETTER WORD (continued)

If you love your job, quality customer service will follow. For the sake of your paycheck, your job, remember: Quality is a four-letter word. LOVE.

Exercise: Quality Is A Four-Letter Word

1. Why shouldn't we consider quality as "frosting on the cake"?

____

____

2. Why is a job important to our well-being?

____

____

3. When you love your job, why is quality customer service automatic?

____

____

Receptionist

A receptionist is an important ambassador or representative of a company. As a receptionist, you have much more credibility and influence than you may realize. Concentrate on being positive, professional and pleasant, and you'll always be proud of what you do—and that will tell your customers that your company's services or products are worth consideration.

Rushing Callers

see also "Six Cardinal Rules of Customer Service"

Always take time with callers; rushing threatens them!

Let's face it … most phone calls we receive are an interruption. Chances are, you don't get much chance to sit around and *wait* for the phone to ring. Therefore, when you answer a phone call, you may rush the caller because *you're* busy. This can be threatening or annoying to the caller.

Give your full attention to the caller. Unless it pertains to the conversation 100 percent, don't write, type, or talk to anyone else besides the caller.

Avoid giving quick, short, rushed answers, which are also intimidating.

Here are a few quick, short answers that make people feel rushed. Try not to use them:

Okay	Sure	Yes
Yeah	Uh-huh	No

RUSHING CALLERS (continued)

Exercise: Rushing Callers

1. What other short answers can you think of? List them here.

____

____

2. Write down some other, more helpful short answers that assure the caller you are listening. (Keep this list by your phone.)

____

____

HE DOESN'T LOOK READY TO TAKE TIME WITH THIS CALLER!

SECTION

VII

SCREENING CALLS

INBOUND CALLS

Screening calls, at its best, is intimidating for the caller; at its worst, screening is humiliating. There are three types of screens that threaten: a single, a double and a triple. Here are examples:

1. **Single Screen:** "Who's calling?"

2. **Double Screen:** "Who's calling, and what company are you with?"

3. **Triple Screen:** "Who's calling? What company are you with? What's this in reference to?"

The person screening might as well be wearing a helmet and holding a rifle. It sounds as though they're interrogating a prisoner!

You may have been instructed to use the following call-screening questions: "Can I ask who's calling?" or "May I tell him/her who's calling?" Even these screens, however, can still offend the caller, because you are putting them through a procedure that may feel threatening.

Telephone "Doctor"®'s recommended, improved screening process is simple. It is a *two-step process* and involves the person doing the screening as well as the person for whom you're screening. If you are asked to screen telephone calls you'll need to share this technique with that person.

SCENARIO #1:

Caller: *"Mr. Lurk, please."*

You: *"Thank you. I'll ring his office.* ***Let me*** *tell him who's calling, please."*

First, it's important to let the caller know *in advance* if the called party is there or not. Never screen the call and *then* tell the caller the party is not available. Secondly, the Let Me technique is far less offensive than "Can I" or "May I tell him who's calling?" Let's continue:

Caller: *"Yes, it's Rebecca Smith."*

You: *"Thanks, Ms. Smith. I'll ring his office."* (Always use the caller's name after the screen.)

SCREENING CALLS (continued)

Then ring Mr. Lark, or otherwise let him know that Ms. Smith is on the line. Now, Mr. Lark *must pick up the call using the caller's name.* Otherwise, don't screen!

Remember, we screen for identification, not elimination! We screen to *personalize* the telephone call. There's little value to screening a call if the person called picks up the phone with "Hello?" If you subject the caller to the screening scenario, make sure they know you're going to use the information.

SCENARIO #2:

Caller: *"Is Irene in?"*

You: *"Yes. I'll ring her office. Let me tell her who's calling, please."* OR

You: *"Irene isn't in the office now; she'll be back at 3:00. My name is Chris. I'm her assistant; how can I help you? What can I do for you?"*

This screening method has several advantages. It creates credibility and redirects the conversation, and the caller still gets helped.

Here's another screening situation to be prepared for. What do you do with calls the boss doesn't want to take? Especially after screening them? For instance, what if your boss says, "Find out who it is and then I'll decide if I'll take the call."

Let's take first things first: There is a better technique than lying. Not many of us would get hired if, in our interview, we said with a smile, "Yes, I'm Sue, and I'm an excellent liar." And few bosses would get on the phone and say to a caller, "Hi, it's me—and I'm not here right now."

However, in this less-than-perfect world, you need a technique for managing this situation. Suppose you take a call, screen it, get the caller's name, and tell the boss who it is. Then you hear: *"Tell 'em I'm not here."*

Here's a technique—instead of lying—that will make you look and feel good. Tell the caller, *"Mr. Lark, Ms. Francis is unavailable. My name is Chris. I'm her secretary* (or assistant, whatever title you have). *How can I help you? What can I do for you?"*

What you have done here is take control of the conversation and offer a truthful diversion. You have taken responsibility for the call, and by using the Service Statement, you're a hero!

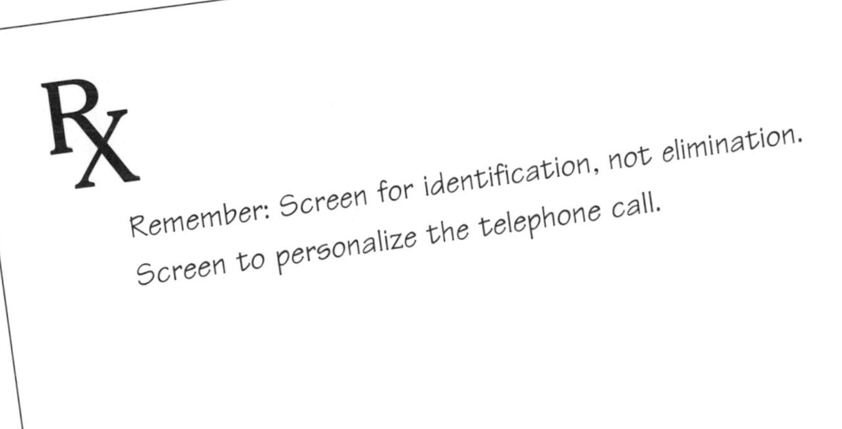

Exercise: Screening Calls (Inbound)

1. Name the three types of screens.

____

____

2. What's the two-step process that makes screening incoming calls less offensive?

____

____

3. Why is it preferable to screen for information, not elimination?

____

____

4. How can you avoid lying when screening incoming calls?

____

____

SCREENING CALLS (continued)

GETTING *PAST* THE SCREEN

Wouldn't it be wonderful if every caller identified him- or herself to you right away? We'd never have to screen a call again! Unfortunately, that's not the way things work most of the time. So when *you* make a telephone call, here's the recommended Telelphone "Doctor"® method. Use it, and you won't get screened. There are three statements you need to make when you make the call:

1. *"This is Jordan Smith …"*
2. *"… with XYZ Company, St. Louis, Missouri."*
3. *"I need to speak with Gerry Sparks."*

When you give this full-disclosure statement at the beginning of the call, you'll seldom get screened. You've done most of the work for the person answering the phone. They'll help you because you've helped them. It works!

Sometimes the person taking the call will still ask, even after you've delivered the full disclosure statement, "And what is this in regard to?" Take a one- or two-second theatrical pause, and say simply, "I'm interested in doing business with your company." It'll get you through almost every time.

Exercise: Screening Calls (Getting Past the Screen)

1. What can you do to avoid being screened?

____

____

2. Why does the full disclosure statement eliminate the third part of the triple screen?

____

____

3. What is the ultimate answer to "And what is this in regard to?"

____

____

SIX CARDINAL RULES OF CUSTOMER SERVICE

Be sure to read these sections:

- **BE FRIENDLY BEFORE YOU KNOW WHO IT IS**
- **COMPANY JARGON**
- **DON'T BE TOO BUSY TO BE NICE**
- **PEOPLE BEFORE PAPERWORK!**
- **PLEASE ... THANK YOU ... YOU'RE WELCOME**
- **RUSHING CALLERS**

SLOW TALKERS

Slow talkers, like fast talkers, can be aggravating. Here's a technique that works wonders with slow talkers when they're stumbling and stammering, trying to ask for what they need.

Caller: "Yes, I'm looking for … um, um, I ah …"

You interject: "Are you calling for Abby, Drew, or Dana?"

It's called the multiple-choice technique. You simply prompt the caller with three or four choices to help them decide what they might need. Here's another example: *"Did you need to change or add to your order?"* They'll fill in the blanks for you.

SLOW TALKERS (continued)

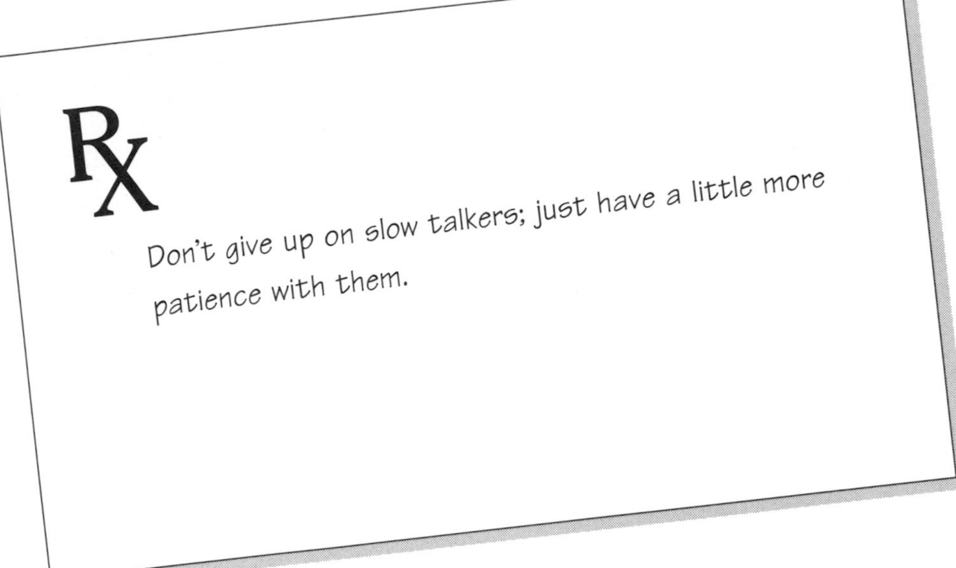

SMILE

Perhaps at a seminar or presentation on telephone skills, you've been told, "You need to smile when you're on the telephone." Telephone "Doctor"® says that's only half right. It's even better to smile BEFORE you pick up the telephone! Be friendly before you know who it is. Afterward, it may be too late. Can you "hear" a smile? Of course you can. You will find it's difficult to be rude when you're smiling. It clearly changes the tone of your voice.

It takes only 17 muscles to smile but 43 muscles to frown. (Get the point?)

Exercise: Smile

1. When is the best time to smile when answering a call?

____

____

2. Why do you believe that you can "hear" a smile?

____

____

3. What's the value of a mirror on the desk?

____

____

Speakerphones

Speakerphones should not be used during initial greetings on incoming *or* outgoing phone conversations. Don't use a speakerphone until you have asked for permission. Try this:

"Excuse me, Ms. Martin. I need to get up and look for some files while we're talking. Do you mind if I put you on the speakerphone?

That's the courteous thing to do. When somebody talks on a speakerphone without asking permission, the person on the other end of the call may infer that someone else is listening in. So don't initiate a conversation over a speakerphone.

And how do you get someone *off* a speakerphone? The quality of a conversation on a speakerphone is often intermittent. Tell the truth. Try this Telephone "Doctor"® technique; it usually works:

"Excuse me, Ms. Martin, I'm having a difficult time understanding you. If you're ***Able*** *to pick up the receiver, I'd appreciate it."*

Speakerphones do have value; for example, at conference meetings. When they are used in this way, the participants need to follow some simple ground rules. If there are more than two people in the room with the speakerphone, each person should identify him- or herself before speaking. And when working with a group who is on the speakerphone, you should identify to whom you are directing your question or comment.

Another fine use of a speakerphone is this: If you're on hold waiting for someone, put the call on your speakerphone. With your hands free, you can do other jobs on your desk—answering or reading memos, opening your mail, and so forth. When your party comes on the line, start out by saying, "Just a moment, let me take you off the speakerphone." Then go ahead with your conversation. This lets you put your time spent on hold to a valuable use.

Exercise: Speakerphones

1. When should you *never* use speakerphones?

____

____

2. What are the ground rules for using speakerphones?

____

____

3. When is the best time for using a speakerphone?

____

____

SWEAR-STOPPERS

see also "Irate Callers"

It is no fun to have someone yell at you, let alone have someone swear at you. And it's not right, either. Unfortunately, there are people who haven't learned that yet. So we need to learn how to deal with them.

Point #1: Never argue with a caller. Don't get into the ring with them. Don't go one round. You will lose every time.

Point #2: When the caller starts to use abusive, foul language, interject—yes, with a smile; that's going to be the key—this swear-stopper: "Excuse me, I can handle your problem ... that's no problem. I cannot handle your abusive language."

Most people do not realize they are swearing. And when you bring it to their attention in an unthreatening manner, it is much easier for them to take.

SWEAR-STOPPERS (continued)

For us to say,

"Stop swearing at me."

will usually get you the following reply:

"You think I'm swearing at you. I'll show you what swearing is ..."

Nine times out of ten, they will apologize for swearing and will tell you how frustrated they are with the situation.

This is the perfect time to use the ASAP technique shown in the Irate Caller section.

℞

Remember the old adage, "You get more with sugar than you do with vinegar."

SWITCHBOARD OPERATOR

see also "Receptionist"

Switchboard operators have one of the most harrying, hurried, hassle-filled positions in any company. Not everyone can be a good switchboard operator. It takes dedication. Unfortunately, these unique, talented people are often underpaid and underappreciated.

As the company "greeter," the goodwill ambassador, the operator sends a signal of what the company is all about. This person helps set the mood for the rest of the call. That's why training in this position is so vitally important.

TRUE TELEPHONE TALES

A personnel agency's client once asked for some tips on finding a good switchboard operator. At that time, his practice was to write an ad, place it in the newspaper and use the P.O. box to avoid a lot of calls. The resumes were reviewed and then the applicants were scheduled for interview appointments. They would take a spelling test, a typing test, and a math test. When asked, "What about the voice test?" the client said, "What voice test?"

It's important to consider the voice qualities of the person who will be first to answer the calls that come into a business. When you're filling any position that requires heavy telephone usage, do the first interview by telephone!

SWITCHBOARD OPERATOR (continued)

Exercise: Switchboard Operator

1. What is the value of the switchboard operator?

   ____

   ____

2. Why is training important for switchboard operators?

   ____

   ____

3. Why should the first interview for a switchboard operator be made on the telephone?

   ____

   ____

THREE-PART GREETING

When you answer a telephone call, the first four to six seconds are critical—because that's all the time you get to make a good first impression on the telephone. As basic and simple as that sounds, if the initial greeting in a phone call is ineffective, the opportunity to create immediate goodwill for a business is lost.

To create a good impression when initially greeting a caller, Telephone "Doctor"® suggests this three-part approach:

1. THE BUFFER

That's the welcoming mat that ushers the caller into your business. *"Good morning." "Good afternoon." "We're glad you called."* Anything that says "thanks for calling." Buffer words set up the most important part of the conversation, which comes next: your company or department name.

Without the buffer words, your company or department name might come across as curt, hard and cold. It's not a disaster if buffer words get cut off, but your company and department name should never be. Have you ever called a company and heard "—ank . . ." when what they really said was "First National Bank"? If the right phone button isn't pushed in time, or the mouthpiece isn't exactly at the person's mouth, part of the company name can get cut off. So add those buffer words to your opening greeting; they are expendable, but company names are not.

2. COMPANY OR DEPARTMENT NAME

After the important buffer words, company or department names should be said confidently and clearly—not rushed, mumbled, or run together.

3. YOUR NAME

Stating your name helps speed the rapport-building process. When a caller has to ask, "Who's this?", it means you've answered the phone ineffectively. And ineffective initial greetings can cost your business many dollars.

THREE-PART GREETING (continued)

An expert initial greeting will create goodwill and start the conversation off on the right foot. Mix together the three parts of the Telephone "Doctor"® recommended greeting and serve them with a big smile: *"Good morning, XYZ Company, this is Steve."*

Then stop. (Remember, in the initial greeting, anything you say immediately after your name may erase your name from the caller's memory.) ("How can I help you?" *is not necessary in the initial greeting*. It is not wrong, merely not necessary. "How can I help you" is best used in message-taking situations.)

For more information about the Service Statement "How can I help you?" see "Message Taking #1 and #2."

℞ Use the Telephone "Doctor"® This Is technique in your three-part greeting: "This is Betty."

Don't say "Betty speaking." Betty Speaking is married to Bob Speaking. They have two children, Judy Speaking and Billy Speaking.

People remember the last thing they hear, so let that be your name, not "speaking."

Exercise: Three-Part Greeting

1. Name the three parts of a greeting to a caller.

   ____

   ____

2. Why is the buffer important?

   ____

   ____

3. What does giving your name achieve?

   ____

   ____

4. Why are effective initial greetings important?

   ____

   ____

TONE OF VOICE

In person, you're like a television set. You have sight, sound, color and motion. On the telephone, you're like a radio. All you have is voice, tone of voice, and the listener's imagination.

The tone of your voice is especially important on the telephone, because it's the key indicator of your emotional state. In person, facial expression and body language are part of the signals you send, along with tone of voice. On the telephone, however, it's like listening to the radio: no visual signals. So the tone of your voice assumes a greater role, as a signaling device.

TONE OF VOICE (continued)

There are a number of ways you can change the meaning of a sentence, just by emphasizing one word or another. Example: "I won't be working today." This sentence can have a different meaning, depending on which of the five words you emphasize. Let's test this with tone of voice. Try reading this sentence aloud, adding in the following emotions or feelings:

ANGRY: "I won't be working today."

BORED: "I won't be working today."

CONFIDENT: "I won't be working today."

HAPPY AND SMILING: "I won't be working today."

Notice that the same words have different meanings with each tone of voice. So you need to remember, again, our strong recommendation: Smile *before* you pick up the phone, and continue to smile while you talk on the phone. It welcomes the caller and sets the stage for positive, productive communication.

TRANSFERRING CALLS

see also "Irate Callers"

℞

Transfer the problem along with the caller. Don't just dump the call to someone else. Let the person who will handle the problem know what's coming.

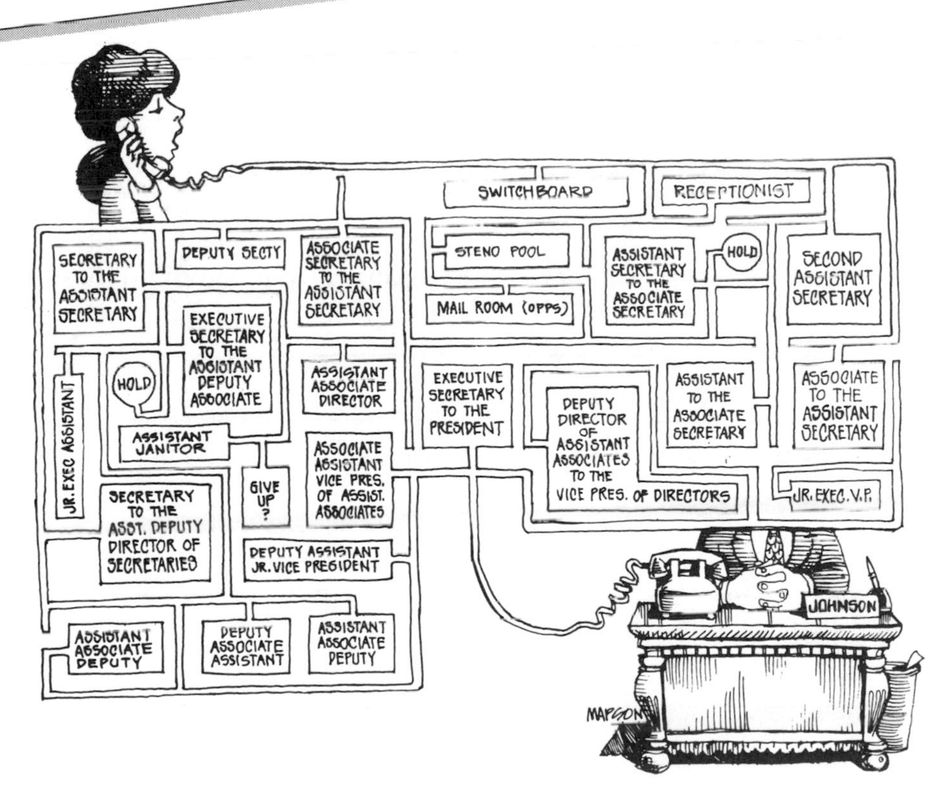

UNAVOIDABLE DELAYS IN ANSWERING

Should you answer the phone in three rings? Yes, certainly, if it's possible. But what happens when it's not possible? That may occur a lot when you're busy, or in an office alone.

When you've answered a phone that has rung more than a few times, use this special Telephone "Doctor"® buffer:

"I'm sorry it rang so long. XYZ Company, this is Victoria." OR

"I'm sorry it rang so long, Mr. Lee's office. This is Jerry."

This greeting accomplishes two things:

- It provides an immediate apology.
- It helps defuse the caller's frustration.

When you feel uncomfortable with the number of times the telephone has rung and it's your turn to answer it, let your buffer words be the apology, rather than ignoring the delay altogether. It doesn't make the situation right, but it does ease the pain.

Exercise: Unavoidable Delays in Answering

1. What's more important than answering the phone within three rings?

____

____

2. Why is it important to have a special buffer for these unavoidable delays?

____

____

3. What does it accomplish?

____

____

SECTION

VOICE MAIL

Answering machines have been with us for awhile, and now voice mail has arrived on the scene, to add to the possible frustration of telephone calls—unless you use these communication tools to your advantage. Voice mail can be a major productivity enhancer for your business and/or personal life. Use it effectively, and it can help you do a better job. Its applications are growing and helping busy people work faster and better. It's important for all business people to know how to use voice mail effectively.

On voice mail, automated attendants have replaced live switchboard operators. These robotic voices start out in a stilted monotone, saying something like this:

> "Thank you for calling XYZ. If you know your party's extension, please press it now. If you're using a rotary phone, please stay on the line and an operator will help you, or press zero to reach the operator."

VOICE MAIL: YOUR SYSTEM

If your company has voice mail with an impersonal automated message, and the attendant's voice is robotic and stilted, consider replacing the automated attendant with a recording of a happy, smiling voice and a more helpful message. You're not obligated to use the voice that came with the voice mail service. It's a good idea to use someone within the company, or you may want to hire a professional "voice."

For your own personal greeting on a voice mail system, here are some tips:

Tip #1: Create your own greeting, rather than using the script and the voice that comes with the system.

Write and record a greeting for your own voice mail box. Be sure to let your personality come through when you record (and yes, smile!). Put some thought and effort into what you say and how you say it. Write out two or three messages, about ten to twelve seconds in length. Put some style into it! Sound like a human, not a machine!

Audit your recording. Then record it over and over again, until you sound conversational, just as though you were speaking face-to-face with a friend. Don't forget to smile all the way through your recording. No one wants to listen to a gruff or bored-sounding voice. Remember, you're representing yourself as well as the company, so make it good.

VOICE MAIL (continued)

Tip #2: Provide all the information that the caller needs.

Voice mail greetings should be concise, but not abrupt. In an effective voice mail greeting, be sure to include your name, title or department (if that's appropriate), and a statement that you're on the phone or away from your desk, at a meeting, out for the day, out of town, whatever. (Again, smile while you're recording!) If you check your messages often (and most of us do … or, at least, should) tell your callers that. More importantly, tell them when you will get back to them. Callers are more willing to leave messages when they know approximately when they can expect a return call.

Tip #3: Always give the caller instructions about how to reach a live voice.

One major complaint about voice mail is that one is rarely given an option beyond leaving a message. It confines the caller to "voice mail jail." If possible, always include in your greeting instructions on how to reach someone—an associate, an assistant, or the operator—for more immediate help.

Tip #4: Update your voice mail greeting often.

If you're going to be out of the office for awhile, perhaps on vacation, in an all-day meeting or on a business trip, let your callers know. Don't lose an important client by not providing enough information about your absence. Remember, always give your callers the number or extension of someone else to call, or some other "escape route" for when you're not available. Here's an example:

"Hi, this is Lisa. I'm in Los Angeles for a sales presentation. I'll be back in the office on Thursday, June 9th. I check my messages often, so please leave a detailed message and I'll get back to you by the end of the day, or press 16 and you can talk to Jeannie, or zero for the operator. Thanks for calling. Have a great day!"

Tip #5: And yes, SMILE while you're recording your message.

Exercise: Voice Mail (Your System)

1. What's the advantage of recording your own greeting rather than using the script/voice that come with the system?

2. What information should you include on your greeting?

3. How do you avoid "voice mail jail?"

4. When should you update your voice mail greeting?

MAYBE IT'S TIME TO TAKE A CLOSER LOOK AT YOUR VOICE MAIL GREETING.

VOICE MAIL: THEIR SYSTEM

It was just a few years ago (before voice mail) that leaving a detailed message was difficult. Business switchboard operators and assistants usually managed to write down one word for every three you dictated, and message takers were sometimes just plain uncooperative. Now we have the opportunity to leave detailed, verbatim messages for the called party, by using voice mail and using it better.

Since about 70 percent of business phone calls contain one-way information, voice mail is an ideal tool. The trick is to use it well. So here are a few suggestions:

1. Interestingly enough, many people are still unaware that the minute you hear the *Th* in *Thank you* and you don't want to bother with automated attendant, you can go ahead and press zero right then. It will bypass and override that robotic message and get you to an operator. (I don't like to say *live* operator, because I've never talked to a *dead* operator.) Or, if you know the extension number, you can also press that right away; this gets you right to your party.

2. Expect your called party not to be available. Have your voice mail message planned out in advance. Only 25 percent of business calls reach the intended party on the first try, so be ready to leave a message.

3. Be friendly, and smile while you're recording your message.

4. *Speak* the message; don't sound like you're reading it. Compose your messages for the ear, not the eye. Use contractions. For example, rather than "I will be calling you," say *"I'll be calling you."*

5. Request a specific call-back time. *"I need to hear from you by 4:00 P.M. or before."* Avoid requests such as "Call me as soon as you can" or "when you have a few minutes." For best results, be specific.

Exercise: Voice Mail (Their System)

1. Why is voice mail an improvement over leaving a message with a person?

___

___

2. How often are calls completed on the first try?

___

___

3. Why is leaving a call-back time important?

___

___

VOICE MAIL: GENERAL TIPS

Voice mail is intended to help people communicate better. Learn to use voice mail enthusiastically, and to your advantage. Here are some general suggestions from Telephone "Doctor"®:

1. Write your own outgoing greeting.
2. Include in your greeting the main points the caller needs to hear, such as your name and when you'll return.
3. Practice delivering your greeting out loud several times before recording, so you'll sound conversational, not stiff.
4. Speak confidently and clearly.
5. Listen to your recording one last time; do you like it? Or should it be re-recorded?

VOICE MAIL: GENERAL TIPS (continued)

6. Remember that your recorded voice will sound "different" to you.

7. Include instructions on how to reach a live person. (Some companies have guidelines and policies governing this, so callers don't end up in "voice mail jail.")

8. State when you'll return, as exactly as possible.

9. Smile *before* you start recording.

10. If the party you're calling is unavailable, ask the operator if they have voice mail, and then use it to your advantage to leave a verbatim message.

Rx

Approximately two-thirds of business communications contain one-way information. Voice mail is ideal for that.

WE ARE CUSTOMERS TO EACH OTHER

Why is it that "inside calls" are often treated differently? In many organizations, the ring of the telephone indicates an inside call—for instance, short rings rather than long ones. These are sometimes answered with a brisk "Yeah?" But it makes good sense to answer the telephone the same way all the time. Callers from inside your company deserve the same professional treatment that you give to outside callers!

Customer service is a high priority with most companies, and Telephone "Doctor"® believes that this sense of good service must start from within. If high-quality service is not practiced within, it will probably not get out over the phone lines to customers and clients.

The three-part greeting you read about earlier is good for inside calls, too: *"Good morning, Accounting. This is Steve."*

Remember, we are customers to each other.

Exercise: We Are Customers to Each Other

1. How should in-house calls be treated?

____

____

2. Why does customer service begin within an organization?

____

____

WE CAN'T DO THAT

see also "Five Forbidden Phrases"

This phrase is guaranteed to get your customer's blood boiling. To many people, it's a challenge. Why challenge someone to find a competitor who *can* do that? Try this instead: "Gee, that's a tough one. Let's see what we can do." Then find a solution.

Never repeat the negative. There's no need to remind the caller of what you *can't* do. Much of the time, you'll find an acceptable positive alternative.

When you have to, how do you let them down gently? Use the Telephone "Doctor"®'s Wish statement:

> *"I wish we could, Mr. Avery. That would be great. However, it's simply not available. It's a great idea, though. What else can we think of?"*

The Wish statement shows callers you've been listening. And that you agree (that's very important). You've acknowledged their need or idea, yet told them you can't help them realize it. But you still didn't say, "We can't do that."

WE CAN'T DO THAT. NOPE, CAN'T DO THAT EITHER. THE "QUICK FIX ORGANIZER COMPANY" ... WHY DO YOU ASK?

WELCOME GUEST

see also "Three-Part Greeting"

℞

When your front doorbell rings, and you open it to find an old friend, you welcome them in, don't you? Let's do the same thing with our business callers. Welcome them in. Make every caller a welcome guest.

X-RATED

An X-rating brands a company as a place never to do business again. X-rated companies don't last long. By treating their customers with an uncaring attitude, these companies guarantee that folks will look for someplace else to patronize for getting their hair cut, their printing done, their car repaired, or obtaining legal advice.

When clients are not treated properly, they go elsewhere. Don't make the mistake of encouraging an X-rated reputation for your company. That makes the competition a little stronger and your company a little weaker. So do everything you can to keep that from happening.

X-RATED (continued)

TRUE TELEPHONE TALES

A mother, shopping by phone for her daughter's wedding shower present, was looking for some fancy bathroom tissue with writing on it. She reached a store that might carry it. She introduced herself with, "Hi, my name is Julia. I'm trying to locate some unusual bathroom tissue paper. It has writing on it." The clerk replied, very coldly, "We don't have any."

In a second effort, Mom said with a big smile in her voice, "You know the kind I'm looking for ... it says Happy Birthday or Congratulations or something fun on it." The clerk bluntly again repeated "I said, we don't have any." And with that, the clerk branded his store as X-rated in the mind of the mother looking for a gift. Neither she nor her friends and associates whom she told about the experience would ever shop there again.

Exercise: X-Rated

1. Name three businesses that have earned your X-rating.

____

____

2. What did they do that cost them your business?

____

____

3. How many people did you tell about the poor treatment you received?

____

____

4. Picking the worst of your three X-rated businesses, what should they have done differently? List *at least* two things.

____

____

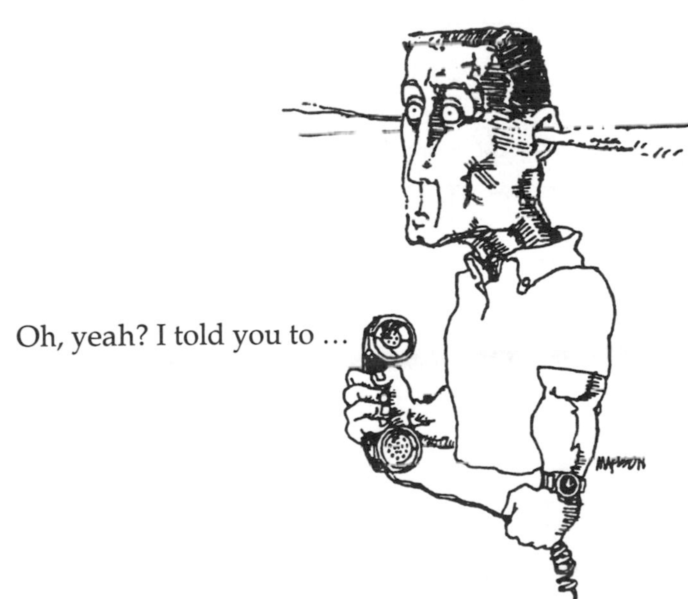

SECTION

IX

"YOU'LL HAVE TO ..."

see also "Five Forbidden Phrases"

"You'll have to ..."

Wrong. The only thing that the caller *has* to do is die and pay taxes. Tell the caller what he or she has to do, and the caller often won't do it. People don't like to be ordered around.

Instead, use phrases such as these:

- "You'll need to ..."
- "Here's how we can help with that."
- "The next time that happens, here's what you can do."

Zest

The dictionary defines *zest* as "stimulating or exciting quality. Keen enjoyment; gusto"—for example: a zest for life.

This book started with *A* for Attitude. Now here we are at *Z* for Zest! We hope we've helped you improve your telephone skills and customer service abilities. The idea is for you to be very good at what you do. To have a zest for helping people.

It's fun to be good at your job. And that will help you have a zest for your job and your life.

"The telephone is your theater, your stage. Your receiver is your curtain. When it goes up, make yourself a star."

—*Nancy Friedman,* President
Telephone "Doctor"®

SECTION

X

INDEX

INDEX (continued)

NOTES

NOTES